LIZ CURTIS HIGGS

Really Bad Girls of the Bible

More Lessons from Less-Than-Perfect Women

WATERBROOK
PRESS

REALLY BAD GIRLS OF THE BIBLE WORKBOOK
PUBLISHED BY WATERBROOK PRESS
12265 Oracle Boulevard, Suite 200
Colorado Springs, Colorado 80921

ISBN: 978-1-57856-546-7

Published in the United States by WaterBrook Multnomah, an imprint of the Crown Publishing Group, a division of Random House Inc., New York.

WATERBROOK and its deer colophon are registered trademarks of Random House Inc.

Printed in the United States of America
2011

Contents

Here We Go Again, Babe

S o glad you're here!

It could be you've already read the book *Really Bad Girls of the Bible* and are eager to learn more about those eight (in)famous women…and more about your own spiritual self in the process. Great, sis! I wrote this workbook with you and your quiet time with God in mind.

Or maybe you're planning on gathering with a bunch of girlfriends to study *Really Bad Girls,* chapter by chapter, and these are the questions you'll be preparing for each week's get-together. Glad to hear it! Through the pages of this workbook, I'll be right there with you, encouraging us all to embrace the boundless grace and utter sovereignty of God.

Here's what I'd suggest: Read the entire corresponding chapter in the book *Really Bad Girls of the Bible* straight through before you do anything else. The contemporary fiction gives us a way to connect with these women; the verse-by-verse nonfiction lets us look at their biblical stories in small sections so we can process it better. The questions at the end of each chapter of the main book are included in this workbook (some have been expanded, others improved!), with space for writing answers, taking notes, or whatever works best for you.

Instead of trying to tackle all the workbook questions in each chapter in one sitting, why not answer one question per day and let the lessons you've learned in those few minutes really sink in? Seven questions, seven days…hey, it works! Whenever you have one of those "aha" moments, jot down that realization under question 8, which is always "What's the most important lesson you learned…?" By week's end, you'll be all set for your group meeting or ready to move on to the next chapter.

Judging by the letters and e-mails rolling in, I'm finding that *Bad Girls of the Bible* and her "younger sister," *Really Bad Girls of the Bible,* have been embraced by women of all ages, all stages, and all walks of life. (Thank you, Lord!) From dorm rooms to prison cells, nursing homes to mom's play groups, women all over the world are discovering how much they have in common with these shadowy sisters from another time and place. Your enthusiasm and vision for how to apply these truths in your own life and share them with others has blessed the socks right off my size-10 tootsies.

Now…are you ready to dive in and let the Lord teach you something new? In addition to this personal workbook, you'll need: (1) your own copy of the book *Really Bad Girls of the Bible,* (2) your favorite Bible (any translation is fine—I used the New International Version), and (3) your favorite pen. Don't worry about putting down the incorrect answer. There's no such thing as "wrong" when you're learning.

Whatever you do, bring a heart willing to be changed and a mind willing to be stretched, because our God has something amazing planned for *you!*

"Thanks for helping a bunch of ordinary moms see the women in the Bible through a different set of eyes. During the first few minutes of our time together, we all share the 'funny things' in the chapter. Somehow having a good laugh first gets us all ready to settle down and dig deeper. The fictional stories grabbed us instantly. We couldn't put our books down! Everyone has agreed your approach is fabulous. We have met women we would have skipped over in Scripture and found them to be women we don't want to emulate. To have this Bible study with these friends and new sisters in the Lord is amazing. You've helped us all grow in our walk with the Lord."

Judy from Michigan

Dead Man Talking

Medium of En Dor

I wrote the opening story of Dora on a dark, wind-swept Friday night when my family was out of town and our old farmhouse was empty. Too empty. By the time I finished, every light in the place was blazing! You, too, might want to turn on a few more lights as you approach this ghostly story about a woman who dabbled in darkness at the bidding of a doomed king.

1a. Check out the first half of **1 Samuel 15:23.** Words like "sin" and "evil" make it clear what God thinks of our Really Bad Girl's "medium-size" activity. Is the fact that God says in his Word, "don't do it," enough to motivate you to stay away from horoscopes, psychics, tarot cards, and the like? Why or why not?

b. Have you ever been drawn—even a little—to such activities? Which ones have the most appeal, and why?

c. People often consider fortune-telling pursuits nothing more than harmless entertainment. Yet God's Word makes it clear they are not to be tolerated. In **1 Samuel 12:14-15** the prophet Samuel clearly stated what is good…and what is not! Note those phrases here:

GOOD (VERSE 14)   NOT GOOD (VERSE 15)

d. Jot down what the following verses teach us about a rebellious nature.

Job 24:13

Psalm 107:17

e. For some of us, rebelliousness came early in our lives. How might the plea of King David in **Psalm 25:7** apply to your own life?

f. For those of us who have children, what does **Deuteronomy 4:9** caution us to do?

g. When it comes to our kids, we might begin with the words of Paul
   in **1 Corinthians 4:14.** How might we equip them to "just say no"
   to séances, Ouija boards, and other spiritually dangerous activities
   that violate God's commands?

Such otherworldly journeys are *forbidden.*

Liz Curtis Higgs in *Really Bad Girls of the Bible,* page 20

2a. Thanks to Shakespeare and many other writers, our visual image of
    a witch is usually an old, toothless hag, huddled over a fire while bats
    circle her gray, stringy hair. Describe your own mental picture of
    a witch.

b. Ever seen or met a modern practitioner of "wicca"—that is, witchcraft? If so, what was your impression?

c. Read **2 Corinthians 11:14-15.** How might Satan's servants masquer-
   ade themselves as servants of righteousness?

d. Why do you think witchcraft has been getting so much positive attention in the movies and other forms of entertainment lately?

e. What makes witchcraft—often simply called, "the craft"—dangerously appealing?

f. Read **2 Timothy 4:3-4.** Do you think that "time" is here and now? If so, what evidence do you see?

g. **Ephesians 4:18** explains how someone could be so misled. What facts stand out to you in that verse?

h. In what ways does that verse describe King Saul's attitude on the last day of his life?

i. Write out the following two verses featured in this chapter.

1 Samuel 28:3b

1 Samuel 28:7a

What discrepancy is obvious here?

j. Describe a time when you've justified a "policy change" in your own life.

k. Is God changeable like Saul was (or like we often are)? Turn to **Psalm 102:25-27** for your answer.

The girl was a rock's throw from disaster.

Liz Curtis Higgs in *Really Bad Girls of the Bible*, page 20

3a. According to **1 Samuel 28:11,** the medium got right to work, friendly and helpful as could be. One pastor, writing in the early years of American spiritualism, claimed to know many mediums as personal friends of trustworthy character. If you count among your friends, acquaintances, or coworkers a woman who dabbles in pursuits identified with the occult, what are those activities?

b. How have you addressed the spiritual danger of such practices with her?

c. Read the apostle Peter's encouragement to the persecuted young church in **1 Peter 2:12.** What does he tell Christians to do when confronted with those who disagree with our beliefs?

d. The apostle Paul's letter to the church at Corinth describes how we are to handle ourselves around unbelievers. Read **2 Corinthians 4:1-4.** In a few words, sum up the teaching found in each verse in your own words:

Verse 1

Verse 2

Verse 3

Verse 4

e. How would you define the "god of this age?" referred to in verse 4?

f. What dangers are present in having friendships with those who dabble in the occult? Is it advisable to walk away from that friendship? Why or why not?

g. What cautionary words do you find in the following verses that might apply to such friendships?

2 Timothy 2:16

Hebrews 2:1

2 Peter 3:17

h. After looking at this subject more closely, do you need to make any changes in your current relationships? If so, describe the steps you need to take.

Darkness and disobedience go together.

Liz Curtis Higgs in *Really Bad Girls of the Bible*, page 24

4a. Read page 14 of *Really Bad Girls of the Bible*. How did Dora describe the positive aspects of her work?

b. In the biblical story, the medium of En Dor didn't slay prophets as
   Jezebel did. Just the opposite. She was obedient, helpful, and generous. She even risked her life to conjure up a *dead* prophet from the
   grave (with a lot of help from God). Do *you* consider her a Really
   Bad Girl? Why or why not?

c. Reread the first page of the fictional account of Dora. When did she
   always meet her customers?

d. Why that time frame, do you think?

e. What does **John 3:20** tell us about light and darkness?

f. How would that verse apply to the medium of En Dor's work?

g. Addressing the Daughter of Babylon—in truth, an entire nation— the prophet Isaiah charged that "woman" with the very sins we've seen in the life of the medium of En Dor. Carefully read **Isaiah 47:10-15.** What two things does this wicked woman say to herself, as recorded in verse 10?

(1)

(2)

h. When might you have mumbled one of those statements under your breath?

i. What evil practices does Isaiah specifically mention?

j. According to verse 11, what will come of such wickedness?

k. What are the counselors described in verse 13, and what common practice does that speak against in our own culture?

l. According to verse 14, what does their future hold?

m. How can you let go of any need to know your own future and simply trust God?

Inside the dark recesses of his soul, a rebellious spark still burned.   Liz Curtis Higgs in *Really Bad Girls of the Bible*, page 21

5a. Read **1 Samuel 28:12-14.** What's your own take on why the medium of En Dor screamed?

b. Why do you suppose the medium could see Samuel but Saul could not?

c. Was God rewarding her efforts…or punishing Saul for seeking her out?

d. Continue with the story in **1 Samuel 28:15-19.** How many times did the prophet Samuel use "the LORD" in these verses?

e. Surely a medium, consorting with evil spirits, wouldn't risk saying God's name so boldly, so often? What might that tell us about who was actually doing the talking?

f. Considering that God clearly told his people he found such practices "detestable," what are some possible reasons for this "effective" séance?

g. Was God contradicting his own command? How might you resolve this apparent dilemma?

h. Read **Daniel 2:27-28.** What does Daniel say God can do that those trafficking in the dark arts cannot?

i. At the bottom of page 29 of *Really Bad Girls of the Bible,* you'll see three questions I ask myself when trying to discern God's voice from the Adversary's. Jot those questions here:

(1)

(2)

(3)

j. As always, God's Word is our authority on such matters. Read **1 John 4:2-3.** What does the Spirit of God do that the spirit of the antichrist does *not?*

Our relationship is not with a dead spirit but with a *LIVING CHRIST.*   Liz Curtis Higgs in *Really Bad Girls of the Bible,* page 34

6a. It's clear to me that the medium had nothing to do with Samuel's appearance. It was a miraculous, utterly God-ordained event for a specific purpose: to deliver this final, humbling news to Saul. Read **1 Samuel 28:19** again. What did Samuel explain would happen on the battlefield the next day?

b. If you had foreknowledge of your own death, how would it change the way you lived today?

c. Read **Psalm 39:4.** David wasn't actually asking God to tell him the day he will die. Rather, what did he seem to be asking?

d. According to **Psalm 139:16b,** does the Lord in fact know the exact moment we will die? If so, when was that decided?

e. How might the fact that the Lord knows the number of your days—and you do not—give you peace?

f. At the top of page 33 in *Really Bad Girls of the Bible,* you'll find two questions I call "biggies." Based on all you've learned so far, how would you answer the first one about the Medium of En Dor?

g. On that page you'll also find **1 Chronicles 10:13-14,** which cites four things that Saul did wrong. List them:

(1)

(2)

(3)

(4)

h. Now that second "biggie" of a question: What does the passage from 1 Chronicles tell us about God's response to the four sins above?

The sooner Saul left, the safer she'd be.

Liz Curtis Higgs in *Really Bad Girls of the Bible*, page 31

7a. When Saul heard the bad news, his reaction was much as our own would be: *splat!* Read **1 Samuel 28:20-21.** Without a description of her voice inflection, facial expressions, or body language to help us, it's difficult to know what the medium was trying to communicate. What do you think she meant by reminding Saul of her obedience to him?

b. Say her words aloud the way *you* think she said them. What emotions do you hear between the lines?

c. Read **1 Samuel 28:22-25.** Why does she offer to feed Saul and company?

d. Does the fact that the medium prepared these men a home-cooked meal in the middle of the night change your view of her at all? Why or why not?

e. According to **Romans 14:17-18** what are some things that matter more to God than food and drink?

f. Did the medium's generous hospitality change *God's* view of her, do you suppose? Why or why not?

g. Sometimes we justify sin by telling ourselves, "But I do this and that
    and the other thing, and *those* are good." How can the following
    verses help us choose wisely and put first things first?

Proverbs 31:30

1 Peter 2:16

The goddess didn't die for your sins...Jesus did.

Liz Curtis Higgs in *Really Bad Girls of the Bible*, page 36

8. What's the most important lesson you learned from the shadowy
    figure of the Medium of En Dor?

2

Lethal Weapon

Jael

My, my, isn't this a gruesome tale? It's tempting to skip such stories, violent as they are. But if they're included in God's Word, there's a positive, life-changing lesson to be learned amid all those chariots and tent pegs. The short answer? God is in charge...and we're not!

1a. Let's start our study just before Deborah is introduced so we get the Big Picture. Read **Judges 4:1-3.** Without a godly leader, what happened to the Israelites?

b. What did God do when his people went bad?

c. How long did the Israelites suffer Sisera's oppression before they realized they needed help?

d. And to whom did they cry out?

e. That same pattern is all through the Old Testament: Israel doing evil, which resulted in bondage, then repenting, which resulted in God's rescuing them. You would think God would have wearied of their constant whining to be delivered out of situations they've walked into with their eyes wide open. *Hmmm.* Sound familiar? What does say **Isaiah 46:4** tell us about God's willingness to rescue his people?

f. Jot down an example of an instance in your life when you were aware of God's rescuing you:

g. Now, let's watch God work: Read **Judges 4:4.** What three job titles are given this ancient woman named Deborah?

(1)

(2)

(3)

h. Does the idea of a female prophet make you uneasy? Why or why not?

i. Read **Psalm 135:6** and record any insights that verse offers.

j. What does **Proverbs 8:15-16** tell us about those whom God chooses to honor with leadership roles?

k. Read **Psalm 47:8.** No matter who sits on the earthly throne, who is really in charge?

> The army was helpful, Barak was a bonus, but the battle was God's alone.   Liz Curtis Higgs in *Really Bad Girls of the Bible*, page 50

2a. **Judges 4:4** and **Judges 4:17** name the husbands of the two women in our story, Deborah and Jael. How does the fact that Deborah and Jael were married yet acted independently of their husbands affect your perception of them?

b. If you are married, under what circumstances do you make important decisions without consulting your husband?

c. How might **Proverbs 31:11** address that situation?

d. If you are single, do you feel a need to get a man's opinion before you make major decisions? Why or why not?

e. Married or single, we are called to consult the Lord above all human counsel. **Romans 12:2** gives us a succinct method of seeking God's will on a matter. According to that verse, what is our responsibility?

f. What words are used to describe God's will?

g. **John 7:17-18** gives us a way of discerning if *others* are walking according to God's will. What does Jesus tell us to look for in our leaders?

h. Look at Deborah's statements as recorded in **Judges 4:6; 4:9;** and **4:14.** In each of her recorded pronouncements, who gets the glory for any good deeds done?

i. How can we, in our own roles, be godly leaders like Deborah?

With God in control, victory was a done deal.

Liz Curtis Higgs in *Really Bad Girls of the Bible*, page 50

3a. Time to get ready for battle. Read **Judges 4:7-8.** What does Deborah promise Barak, the commander of the Israelite army, that she will do?

b. Why do you think Barak refused to go into battle without Deborah?

c. Perhaps Barak was just being cautious. How might **Luke 14:31** address this situation?

d. **Judges 4:9** and **Judges 4:10** repeat the same statement, perhaps for emphasis. What is it, and what does this tell you about Deborah?

e. Read Deborah's message to Barak in **Judges 4:14.** What is her command?

f. Barak immediately follows her orders. Why do you suppose he does so?

g. **Psalm 18:39** might suit Deborah well, as would **Psalm 33:16-22.** How might she be a role model for you in serving the Lord on your own daily "battlefronts"?

The Lord will use whom he will, how he will.

Liz Curtis Higgs in *Really Bad Girls of the Bible*, page 61

4a. In **Judges 4:9** Deborah declared, "The LORD will hand Sisera over to a woman." Do you think Deborah meant herself or Jael? Or was she speaking prophetically, not yet understanding how it would be fulfilled?

b. Did the prophets of old—Isaiah, Jeremiah, Hosea, and the rest— decide when to deliver God's messages to his people or what those messages would be? What does **2 Peter 1:20-21** tell us?

c. How can we understand those prophecies? What answer do you find in **1 John 5:20**?

d. Jesus is the embodiment of God's truth as recorded in his Word. What do the following verses tell us about the nature of God's Word and why we can trust it fully?

1 Thessalonians 2:13

Acts 20:32

> [Sisera] was her guest, yes, but the enemy of Yahweh as well.
>
> Liz Curtis Higgs in *Really Bad Girls of the Bible*, page 57

5a. Now let's see how Deborah's prophecy came true. Read **Judges 4:15-17** for details of Sisera's escape from the battlefield. What sort of reception was Sisera expecting at Jael's tent, and why?

b. Read **Judges 4:18-19.** In what ways did Jael make Sisera welcome?

c. Why do you think Jael comforted him with the words, "Don't be afraid?"

d. Sisera, meanwhile, was oblivious to a prophetic truth that was unfolding all around him. He just wanted to take a nap. Read **Judges 4:20.** What did he ask Jael to do?

e. Read **Judges 4:21.** Did she do his bidding?

f. Why do you suppose God allowed Sisera to escape death on the battlefield only to die hours later at the hand of Jael?

g. What does God say in **Psalm 75:2**?

h. How does this story of Deborah's prophecy, which was fulfilled the very same day, build your faith in God?

[Jael] stepped out on faith, on purpose, and without fear.

Liz Curtis Higgs in *Really Bad Girls of the Bible*, page 53

6a. Read the modern account of Jill on pages 46-47 of *Really Bad Girls of the Bible.* Jill was trying to decide whether to pull the trigger, justifying his murder one minute, talking herself out of it the next. After reviewing Jill's arguments and justifications, see if you can come up with a similar list for Jael.

REASONS TO KILL SISERA   **REASONS NOT TO KILL SISERA**

b. Why do you think I didn't finish the fictional story? (Hint: It was not because I ran out of time or paper!)

c. What is the critical difference between these two stories—the fictional and the biblical—that makes all the difference? It's not motive or method. What is it? Think through the possibilities, then consult **1 Timothy 1:17.**

d. If you'd been Jael in that tent and Sisera showed up, do you think you would have been able to kill him, or would you have tried to detain him until Barak or someone else came along? How would you make that decision?

e. How might **Psalm 37:28** assure us that if we're ever in a Jael situation, we will not be alone?

f. Read **Judges 4:22.** Does Jael take credit for killing Sisera at this time?

g. Now read **Judges 4:23** Who actually gets the credit for the Israelite victory that day?

> God...empowered a brave woman with a tent peg to strike a blow for righteousness.
>
> Liz Curtis Higgs in *Really Bad Girls of the Bible,* page 58

7a. No one actually *saw* Jael do the dirty deed, did they? Yet Deborah and Barak sing her praises in Judges 5, so Jael must have confessed what happened and admitted she was responsible. Read **Judges 5:24-27** for Deborah's description of Jael's swift justice. Do you agree that Jael was "most blessed?" Why or why not?

b. Compare the descriptions of the tent peg scene as seen through Jael's eyes in **Judges 4:19,21** and Deborah's eyes in **Judges 5:25-26.** What similarities do you find in both accounts?

c. Now look at **Judges 5:27.** This verse seems to disagree with **Judges 4:21,** which clearly states that Sisera was already stretched out asleep on the ground. Here's the truth: "Fall," "sink," "lay" are all euphemisms for death. Why do you think Deborah goes over the top in her description of Sisera's demise?

d. When it comes to stories like this one, motivation matters. On pages 57-58 in *Really Bad Girls of the Bible,* you'll find a list of six possible reasons why Jael did what she did. Briefly jot down those reasons here:

(1)

(2)

(3)

(4)

(5)

(6)

e. Which items on this list seem godly, and which seem merely selfish or vindictive?

f. Did in fact the end justify the means in this situation? Why or why not?

g. Many a Sarsour—or a Sisera—gets away with murder today without a brave Jael to put a stop to it. How do the words of the Lord recorded in **Deuteronomy 32:35** assure us that cruel, ungodly people have a tent peg in their future?

h. While few of us will ever find ourselves in a situation that calls for actions as drastic as Jael's, we all occasionally have opportunities to "take someone down a notch"—someone who, by all accounts, deserves it. How can we be sure our motives are godly rather than selfish or vindictive?

God is in charge. Deal with it.

Liz Curtis Higgs in *Really Bad Girls of the Bible,* page 63

8. What's the most important lesson you learned from the guts-and-glory story of Deborah and Jael?

3

Peculiar Grace

The Adulteress

Oh, Grace. Your story strikes a chord with so many of us who've had our sins dragged into the light of day for the whole world to see. Where would we be without Jesus? He rescued this nameless woman from a certain stoning...and saves us from certain death.

1a. Read the start of our biblical story in **John 8:1-4,** then read **Leviticus 20:10.** If the Pharisees legitimately "caught her in the act," what should have been done to the man?

b. Why didn't that happen, do you suppose?

c. Do you think Jesus would have extended grace to the man as well? Why or why not?

d. Turn to page 74 in *Really Bad Girls of the Bible* for an introduction to our fictional hero, Dr. Frank Consuelo. See how many attributes you can find describing Frank, knowing those same words and phrases also describe our true hero, Jesus.

e. Even Frank's name gives away his personality! Grab a dictionary, and I'll show you what I mean. What's the definition of "frank"?

f. "Consuelo" comes from a Spanish word that means "consolation." What does it mean "to console" someone?

g. How did Jesus' actions toward the biblical adulteress exemplify those traits?

Adultery...breaks the law of God and the law of man.

Liz Curtis Higgs in *Really Bad Girls of the Bible,* page 78

2a. **John 8:3** tells us the woman was forced to stand "before the group."
Public exposure and its resulting humiliation have a long tradition.
Can you give some examples from history—the stocks, the whipping
post, others?

b. What was such punishment meant to accomplish in the life of the
offender?

c. What do you suppose onlookers thought or felt?

d. List any modern examples of public exposition—the tabloids, talk
shows, others?

e. What might be some of our motives, as a society, when we put sin on
public display?

f. It seems that human nature has changed little in two thousand years. Yet when the grace of God enters the scene—then and now—everything changes! Read **John 8:5-7.** How did Jesus extend grace to this woman, even before he formally released her from condemnation?

g. Since, we're called to follow Christ's example, what does **Galatians 6:1** instruct us to do when someone is caught in sin?

She was an object, a pawn in their hands, a means to an end.

Liz Curtis Higgs in *Really Bad Girls of the Bible*, page 80

3a. Read **John 8:5** again. The Pharisees weren't satisfied with mere humiliation; they demanded the death sentence. The first half of **John 8:6** explains their real motive, which was what?

b. The bottom half of page 81 in *Really Bad Girls of the Bible* explains the no-win situation at hand. Consider the outcomes for the two individuals involved. What might happen to Jesus—and to the adulteress—based on how Jesus responded?

CONSEQUENCES FOR JESUS   **FOR THE ADULTERESS**

If Jesus *agreed*
with the Pharisees...

If Jesus *opposed*
the Pharisees...

c. If the teachers of the Law and the Pharisees were supposed to be the Good Guys, upholding the tenets of the faith, let's find out where they went wrong. Read the following verses and note any characteristics of the Pharisees you find.

Matthew 23:27-28

Luke 12:1

Luke 16:14

d. What religious groups today might compare to the Pharisees, and what similarities do you see?

e. Read **Matthew 10:16.** How does Jesus tell us we are to behave among Pharisees?

f. If we aren't careful, we could fall into the same judgmental trap that ensnared the Pharisees. What does **Romans 2:1-3** teach us about judging others?

This nameless woman was silent. The rabbi was quieter still.

Liz Curtis Higgs in *Really Bad Girls of the Bible*, page 80

4a. This is the only New Testament record we have of Jesus writing. Read the second half of **John 8:6.** Since the Bible never explicitly tells us, what do *you* think Jesus wrote in the dust…and why?

b. In **John 8:7** we learn that Jesus silenced the Pharisees by something he *did* and something he *said.*

What did he do?

What did he say?

c. By his definition, who among those present had the right to throw that stone?

d. The words Jesus spoke were, in effect, an invitation: "You may throw the first stone *if…*" Read **John 8:8.** Some scholars say that he was doing nothing more than doodling in the sand to (1) give them time to think things over and to (2) kindly avert his eyes from the exposed woman and avoid adding to her shame. What do *you* think?

e. Whatever he was doing—or writing—it had an effect on the Pharisees. Read **John 8:9.** How did they respond to his "invitation"?

f. How might **Romans 3:19-20** fit this scene in the temple that morning?

g. Can you think of a similar instance in your own life when something written left you feeling undeniably convicted of your sin? What was it…and what was the outcome?

h. Read **Romans 6:21-22.** Who benefited most in this scene—the woman, the Pharisees, or the crowd of onlookers? Try making a case for each one.

BENEFITS RECEIVED THAT MORNING

The Adulteress

The Pharisees

The Onlookers

i. What benefit did *you* receive from reading this story?

With her detractors out of the picture, things were looking up.
Liz Curtis Higgs in *Really Bad Girls of the Bible*, page 86

5a. Now that the Pharisees were gone, things got even more interesting! Note the last phrase in **John 8:9.** Why do you think the adulteress stayed, when the Pharisees who had accused her had left?

b. Read **John 8:10.** Jesus was no longer writing in the sand, nor was he bent down to avoid seeing her. If Jesus did meet her gaze, what might that have communicated to her?

c. What two questions did he ask her?

d. Still have that dictionary handy? What are some of the definitions of the word "condemn"?

e. What did the Law of Moses say about adultery? Write out **Exodus 20:14.**

f. In biblical times, adultery was so serious a crime that it required execution. Why do you think adultery isn't taken more seriously—even by Christians—today?

g. If you knew a Christian friend was committing adultery, would you feel compelled to approach her about her sin? Why or why not?

h. If so, what biblical advice would you give her?

i. How would you handle an adulterous friend who was *not* a Christian? Would your approach be different and, if so, how?

j. Jesus offered a cautionary word about considering ourselves righteous because we've avoided adultery. Read **Matthew 5:27-28.** What do you think Jesus meant?

k. On page 84 of *Really Bad Girls of the Bible,* I list the Seven Deadly Sins. Copy them here.

(1)

(2)

(3)

(4)

(5)

(6)

(7)

Now the hard part: Next to each one, put a word or two to remind you of a particular incident from your own life that would fit that sin. (If you're struggling to find a behavior to suit one of them, see number one on the list!)

l. Though the order is traditional, there's no suggestion that one sin is worse than another. Write out **James 2:10.**

m. What does this mean to you?

The Bible doesn't say "*law* one another"–it says "*love* one another." Liz Curtis Higgs in *Really Bad Girls of the Bible*, page 82

6a. The only words the adulteress speaks in this story are recorded in **John 8:11.** What was her answer to Jesus' question, "Has no one condemned you?"

b. Jesus made two statements in response. One was an action he *would not* do; one was an action she *should* do. Complete these sentences:

He would not…

She should…

c. What qualification, if any, did Jesus add? That is, did he say something like, "I will not condemn you *unless*…" or "I will forgive you *if*…"?

d. In order for this woman to move forward and "leave her life of sin," think of all the relationships that would need mending, the trust that would need to be rebuilt. If you were in her sandals, how might you go about seeking the forgiveness of others?

e. One of the dangers of experiencing victory in some sinful area of our lives is that we turn around and judge others for the very sin we just left behind. (Been there, babe. Have you?) What do the following verses teach us?

Luke 6:37

Colossians 3:12

Colossians 3:13

f. And how do we forgive ourselves when we sin—publicly or privately? Note what these verses remind all of us.

Acts 13:38

Romans 5:1-2

Romans 5:8

g. Go back to section k in question 5, where you bravely listed the Seven Deadly Sins and your own specific sins. Next to each of your sins write this:

"Neither do I condemn you."—*Jesus*

Jesus is...the only man who could have tossed that rock...but he didn't.   Liz Curtis Higgs in *Really Bad Girls of the Bible,* page 84

7a. When we've lived in open rebellion in the past, sometimes the hardest thing about our new life in Christ is to avoid being drawn back into that sinful lifestyle. What does **Romans 6:12-13** tell us we need to do?

b. In what specific ways might you "offer the parts of your body" to God?

c. The temptation to sin sexually is every bit as prevalent now as it was then. How can a godly woman who does *not* have a promiscuous past resist the temptation to find out what she "missed" all those years?

d. How might the following verses encourage all of us, no matter what our past?

Isaiah 43:18-19

Ephesians 1:7-8

Ephesians 2:3-5

The past—hers and ours—isn't the point. The Lord is more interested in our future.   Liz Curtis Higgs in *Really Bad Girls of the Bible*, page 89

8. What's the most important lesson you learned from this nameless, faceless, yet grace-covered adulteress?

4

Blood Will Tell

Athaliah

Ever worked with a woman as despicable as Regina Banks of Atlanta? Women that wicked are rare…but they're out there. Left unchecked by the Holy Spirit, some of us take-charge chicks might not be too far behind Queen B. Rather than hurrying through Athaliah's horrific history, let's lean in closer for a good, long look…in our mirrors.

1a. Athaliah earns her Really Bad Girl crown because of her actions recorded in **2 Chronicles 22:10.** What did she do to the house of Judah?

b. Now read **Proverbs 14:1.** What does a wise woman do?

c. And what does a foolish one do?

d. How might **Habakkuk 2:12** address her situation?

e. This was hardly the first regal bloodbath in Scripture. Who killed whom in **2 Chronicles 21:4**?

f. Did you find Athaliah's actions more loathsome than Jehoram's, simply because she was a woman? Why or why not?

g. Is your answer based on social expectations or biblical ones?

h. How does the fact that she executed her *own grandchildren* affect your feelings about her behavior?

i. We studied Deborah earlier (**Judges 4:4**), a woman who was gifted and called to lead Israel. Both Deborah and Athaliah were strong, courageous, bold, fearless, and unafraid of violence…yet they were very different women indeed! List some of the differences you see between these two female leaders.

JUDGE DEBORAH WAS…   QUEEN ATHALIAH WAS…

j. Consider your own leadership style. Do you identify with either woman? If so, in what ways?

Let God shine a light on that…queen-at-all-costs spirit many of us harbor. Liz Curtis Higgs in *Really Bad Girls of the Bible,* page 109

2a. Open your Bible to **Psalm 10.** Though the psalmist was describing another wicked adversary, this passage gives us an accurate picture of Athaliah as well. Read through the following verses, mentally substituting "her" for "his," "she" for "he," "woman" for "man," etc. Note a word or two for each verse that fits Athaliah to a T, paying particular attention to how this wicked person views God.

Psalm 10:2

Psalm 10:3

Psalm 10:4

Psalm 10:5

Psalm 10:6

Psalm 10:7

Psalm 10:11

b. Can you think of any legitimate reasons for the corrupt Athaliah to have ascended to the throne?

c. How do you suppose she justified her ungodly actions to herself?

d. And how might she have convinced those around her to support her for six long years?

e. Read **2 Chronicles 22:3.** Who encouraged the young Ahaziah to do wrong?

f. **Proverbs 10:17** tells us "whoever ignores correction leads others astray." Describe a time when you might have felt manipulated or "led astray" by an employer or someone else in leadership.

g. Did you bring such manipulation to his or her attention? What was the result of your action or inaction?

h. Why do we sometimes put up with others' manipulation when we know we shouldn't?

i. Whether we confront them or not, sometimes corrupt leaders self-destruct. Read **Proverbs 5:22-23.** In your personal life or in the public arena, have you watched a less-than-virtuous leader have a career meltdown? Think of someone in particular. What happened?

j. How can we learn good lessons from their bad examples?

Queen A takes the prize for Least Sympathetic and Most Despicable.   Liz Curtis Higgs in *Really Bad Girls of the Bible*, page 118

3a. Read pages 102-105 of *Really Bad Girls of the Bible,* where our fictional Regina confronts her daughter, Portia. (*Regina* means "queen," and *Portia* means "an offering.") Jot down a few comments about their apparent view of one another.

REGINA SEES HER DAUGHTER AS...

PORTIA SEES HER MOTHER AS...

b. If you have teenagers under your roof, does the tone of their conversation sound at all familiar to you?

c. Make a check mark next to the above observations about our fictional mom that seem to mirror the biblical Athaliah's weaknesses as a mother. Now put an *X* next to any traits that might describe *you* on occasion. What changes might you need to make in your current relationships with your mother and/or daughter(s)?

d. Read **Ezekiel 16:44-45a.** Though that passage was part of God's long diatribe on the nation of Israel, his words suit Athaliah's story as well. Few mothers in history have been more deadly than Jezebel, few fathers more evil than Ahab. In your opinion, how much did the negative influence of her parents factor into Athaliah's personality and pursuits?

e. Who bears more responsibility for the horrifying outcome of this story: Jezebel for raising her daughter to worship Baal or Athaliah for not seeking out the one true God? What leads you to that conclusion?

f. What does **Psalm 78:2-7** tell us to do concerning our children's spiritual welfare, and what will be the result?

g. **Joshua 24:15** is the oft-quoted verse, "As for me and my household, we will serve the LORD." What significance does that verse have for you?

h. At what point do we allow our children to choose for themselves whom they will serve?

i. Does a parent's influence extend throughout a child's life? If so, in what ways?

j. What about after a parent is deceased? Is she or he still an influence? If so, how?

k. Who in your family lineage may have prayed for you to become a godly woman?

l. If you don't have children of your own, how might you influence the next generation of children in your life?

The men who preceded Athaliah on the throne were equally as violent.   Liz Curtis Higgs in *Really Bad Girls of the Bible*, page 120

4a. Athaliah might never have ascended to the throne if her husband, Jehoram, had not died during his kingship. Read the contents of a letter that King Jehoram received from the prophet Elijah in **2 Chronicles 21:12-15.** Unfortunately, whose influence prevailed in Jehoram's life?

b. What crime did Jehoram commit?

c. And what would be his sentence?

d. In **2 Chronicles 21:18** we learn that "the LORD afflicted Jehoram with an incurable disease." He didn't just get sick; it was the Lord's doing. Is this a difficult concept for you to accept? Why or why not?

e. Read **Job 34:12.** How might this assure you that God's ways are just?

f. Jehoram's youngest son, Ahaziah, followed his father's foul example. Read **2 Chronicles 22:2-4.** How long did Ahaziah reign as king?

g. Where did he turn for approval or advice—to Lord or to his advisers?

h. What influence did those advisers exert on young Ahaziah?

i. Ahaziah's short reign ended abruptly. Read **2 Chronicles 22:7.** Who brought Ahaziah down?

j. The last line of **2 Chronicles 22:9** gives us a hint of what is to come. What does it say about the house of Ahaziah?

A leader succeeds only when surrendered to God.

Liz Curtis Higgs in *Really Bad Girls of the Bible*, page 119

5a. Read **2 Chronicles 22:10** again. Immediately on the heels of that bad news comes good news from a godly woman. Read **2 Chronicles 22:11-12.** Don't let all the names that start with *A* or *J* confuse you—it's their relationships with one another that matter. Which grandson of Queen Athaliah was spared and by whom?

b. What might the fact that Athaliah didn't find out about her surviving grandson all those years tell us about her?

c. And what does it suggest about the people who surrounded her?

d. Read **Psalm 32:7** and **Psalm 64:2.** Think of several advantages Joash might have enjoyed by being raised by his aunt and uncle.

e. **Genesis 50:20** records the words of Joseph, a wronged son whom God redeemed. Can you cite an example from history or current events where God used the bad intentions of men to produce good?

f. Describe a time in your own life when God used a negative experience to bring about a positive end.

Alone and undefended, the ruthless queen Athaliah met her gruesome end. Liz Curtis Higgs in *Really Bad Girls of the Bible*, page 117

6a. Athaliah's story does *not* have a happy ending—not for her, anyway.
   Read **2 Chronicles 23:12.** Where does Athaliah go, and why?

 b. The cheering men were bearing arms. Back up a few verses and read
   2 Chronicles 23:9. What were the men carrying?

 c. To whom had those items belonged?

 d. And where had they been stored?

 e. Queen Athaliah failed to destroy God's worship center, God's
   weaponry, and God's chosen seed. Whose power and authority
   reigned that day, then?

 f. Read **2 Chronicles 24:1-2.** How did Athaliah's grandson Joash
   handle his kingly duties?

g. How long did he reign?

h. What do the following verses teach us about God's plans for wicked folks?

Job 5:12

Isaiah 13:11

i. For those of us who *don't* want to be like Athaliah when we grow up, what instruction do these New Testament teachings offer?

Philippians 2:3

James 3:13-14

Ambition is a nice word for covetousness.

Liz Curtis Higgs in *Really Bad Girls of the Bible,* page 120

7a. Read **Psalm 4:2.** As with her mother, Jezebel, Athaliah's problem
   boiled down to worshiping the wrong god—a common problem
   then and now. Even though Baal worship isn't something we hear
   much about today, we have plenty of false gods all around us. See
   if you can come up with five "idol" possibilities in the life of our
   fictional Regina Banks. A quick skim through pages 95-100 in
   Really Bad Girls of the Bible should do it. Then list five "false gods"
   you find in your own life.

REGINA'S IDOLS	YOUR IDOLS
(1)	(1)
(2)	(2)
(3)	(3)
(4)	(4)
(5)	(5)

b. Idols are a problem for all of us, not just the Athaliahs of history.
   Let's take a look at how Jehoiada handled the idols in Baal's temple.
   Read **2 Chronicles 23:17.** Who went to the temple of Baal and what
   did they do to it?

c. What did they do to the altars, the idols, and the priest of Baal?

d. What does this say to you about "tolerating" idols in our midst?

e. How might you tear down your own list of idols from the altar of your heart as thoroughly as Jehoiada and company did the idols of Baal?

Wicked plans fail. God's plans prevail.
   Liz Curtis Higgs in *Really Bad Girls of the Bible*, page 120

8. What's the most important lesson you learned from the violent life of Athaliah, the only woman who ever ruled alone as queen of Israel?

5

Bathing Beauty

Bathsheba

Your dictionary will tell you that those daytime melodramas we call "soap operas" were so named because their earliest sponsors were manufacturers of soaps, such as Ivory and Palmolive. But we know better. The *first* soap opera aired three thousand years ago when a lovely young lady took a springtime bath and made quite a splash with her viewing audience, King David.

1a. According to **2 Samuel 11:1,** David neglected his kingly duties by hanging around the palace while his men were at war. Have you ever avoided some unpleasant duty then found yourself in trouble? If so, what happened?

 b. Make a list of the "duties" in your life that seem most like drudgery?

c. If these are part of your daily "must do" list, they won't go away! The following verses encourage us to keep our commitments *and* maintain a do-it-for-the-Lord enthusiasm for them. Write down a phrase that captures the message each verse has for you, and identify a particular task you're determined to tackle with a better attitude.

	MESSAGE FOR YOU	YOUR TASK
Romans 12:11		
1 Corinthians 15:58		
Ephesians 6:7-8		

d. Read **2 Samuel 11:2.** Do you think David was *looking* for trouble when he strolled around on his roof? Why or why not?

e. Boredom and routine may find us looking beyond the safety of home for something to pique our interest. Write out **Proverbs 17:24.**

f. When have you been tempted to let your eyes wander? And how did you handle that temptation?

g. What does **Proverbs 16:2** tell us about being innocent?

Our Walking David turned into a Peeping Tom.

Liz Curtis Higgs in *Really Bad Girls of the Bible*, page 135

2a. David surely considered himself innocent of any wrongdoing when he sent his men to inquire about the woman's identity. Read **2 Samuel 11:3.** David's men return to the palace with three important facts about the bathing beauty. List them below:

(1)

(2)

(3)

b. Read **2 Samuel 11:4.** So much for innocence. The facts of their affair are brief and to the point. Skipping the parenthetical phrase for a moment, what four things happened that spring evening as outlined in this verse?

(1) First, David…

(2) So, Bathsheba…

(3) Then, David…

(4) Finally, Bathsheba…

c. David's two sins are obvious. Let's look at Bathsheba's role in this sinful encounter. On pages 141-142 in *Really Bad Girls of the Bible,* read the paragraphs immediately following the headings "Bad to the Bone" and "Had by the Throne." Which phrase do *you* think best describes Bathsheba here?

d. What made you choose the answer you did?

e. Can you think of a time when you were decidedly "bad" *or* definitely "had"? How did the situation make you feel? Guilty? Gullible? Wicked? Wimpy?

f. Even if you were decidedly bad and felt guilty as all get-out, God's Word offers incredible hope. What do these verses tell us about our sin—and God's grace?

Mark 2:16-17

Luke 15:10

1 Timothy 1:15

Never have the words "wrong place, wrong time" fit a situation so snugly.Liz Curtis Higgs in *Really Bad Girls of the Bible*, page 134

3a. David's story so overshadows Bathsheba's, it's easy to miss the lessons she has to teach us, especially without a record of her thoughts or emotions to guide the way. Read **2 Samuel 11:5.** Finally, Bathsheba speaks! And she says what?

b. In what ways might this have been good news, from Bathsheba's viewpoint?

c. Why did she tell David, do you think? What outcome might she have been seeking?

d. It seems Bathsheba discharged the duty of handling this matter completely to David. Why might that have been the case?

e. Above all this story is about taking responsibility for our actions...or facing the consequences. Think back to our story about the woman caught in adultery (**John 8:3-5**). What consequences might Bathsheba have faced as an adulteress?

f. David had other consequences to think about—like her wronged husband. Read **2 Samuel 11:6-7.** After some small talk, David's nefarious plans kicked in, which I called in the book Plan A, Plan B, and Plan C. Do we ever see David seeking God's counsel on any of those plans?

g. What does **Proverbs 16:3** tell us about making plans?

h. Study Plan A, described in **2 Samuel 11:8-11.** How did Uriah unknowingly thwart David's plan?

i. Now review Plan B, outlined in **2 Samuel 11:12-13.** How did Uriah hinder David's plan a second time?

j. Finally, read Plan C in **2 Samuel 11:14-17.** What was David's final (and, unfortunately, successful) scheme against Uriah?

k. Have you ever attempted a simple cover up scheme, only to find yourself piling lie upon lie? What happened?

l. When we realize we've dug ourselves into a pit of sin and regret, **2 Corinthians 7:10-11** shows us the way out. Describe the fruit of godly sorrow in our lives.

David took Uriah's wife and *then* took Uriah's life.

Liz Curtis Higgs in *Really Bad Girls of the Bible,* page 140

4a. Somehow David must have justified these sinful acts—first the Bathsheba affair, then his A-B-C plots against Uriah, the last one ending in murder. What half-truths do you suppose he told himself to ease his conscience?

b. Was it pure rebellion on David's part? Stupidity? A midlife crisis? A power trip? How else might you explain godly King David committing these sinful acts?

c. Think back to the most flagrant example of lust, greed, or covetousness you've committed in recent memory. What was it you wanted—a thing, an activity, a person—and why was it so appealing?

d. How did you convince yourself you deserved it?

e. What elements of this biblical story do you see in your own struggle?

f. What do the following verses teach us about temptation?

2 Corinthians 11:3

James 1:13-14

1 John 2:16

Bad or good, Bathsheba's actions and motives cannot be
changed. *But ours can.*

Liz Curtis Higgs in *Really Bad Girls of the Bible*, page 142

5a. Even if we've never been in a situation as volatile as Bathsheba's, we can
identify with her plight as a woman who felt out of control. Review
page 133 in the fictional story of Bethany and Rex in *Really Bad Girls
of the Bible*. Bethany's defenses gave way to his double-barreled
onslaught on her senses. Make a list of her observations about Rex.

HIS PHYSICAL ATTRACTIVENESS   HIS PERSONAL ATTENTIVENESS

b. Continue reading to the end of the story on page 134. What excuses
did Bethany make for not resisting his advances?

c. How do **Romans 7:18-19** and **Galatians 5:17** describe her conflict-
ing desires?

d. If you were Bathsheba, brought to that opulent palace on a warm spring night, could you have said no to David's invitation?

e. What would have made the idea attractive and hard for you to resist? Or repulsive and easy to reject?

f. And what of Bathsheba—do you think she refused David even for a moment?

g. Review **2 Samuel 11:4.** Did Bathsheba even have the option to refuse him? Why or why not?

h. In **2 Samuel 11:26** she learns the sad news of Uriah's death. Do you think Bathsheba knew anything about Plans A, B, and C? Why or why not?

Uriah's loyalty only served to heighten David's disgrace.

Liz Curtis Higgs in *Really Bad Girls of the Bible*, page 146

6a. Read **2 Samuel 11:27.** Bathsheba came into the royal household, fresh from a time of mourning…and obviously pregnant. How might those early months in the palace with David's other wives— Ahinoam, Abigail, Maacah, Haggith, Abital, Eglah—have unfolded for her?

b. More than one man has been trapped into marrying a woman because their one-night fling was on the wrong night. Bathsheba wasn't ignorant of how her body worked. Is there any chance the whole thing was a setup on her part? Why or why not?

c. Amid wedding bells and nursery rhymes, don't miss the last line of **2 Samuel 11:27.** Write that short sentence here.

d. It was time for God to discipline David. According to **Proverbs 3:11-12,** what was God's *motive* for doing so?

e. God sent the prophet Nathan, like a human paddle, to confront David with his sins. Read Nathan's parable in **2 Samuel 12:1-4,** and identify each real-life counterpart.

The rich man was:

The poor man was:

The ewe was:

The hungry traveler was (hint: see **1 Peter 5:8**!):

f. Perhaps if David had sent that hungry "guest" on his way, instead of inviting trouble through his gaze and then his door, David never would have found himself in this situation. Read **2 Samuel 12:5-6.** What did David think the rich man's sentence should be?

g. How did he think the poor man should be compensated for the lamb?

h. What did David say the rich man *lacked?*

i. Have you ever caught yourself expressing righteous indignation over someone else's offense simply because you're suffering from a guilty conscience? If so, what can we learn from David's mistake?

j. In response, Nathan goes on a rant. Read **2 Samuel 12:7-12.** Write down...

David's Sins   **David's Suffering**

k. In **2 Samuel 12:13** are recorded two simple but amazing statements. Note them below.

David says: "

Nathan says: "

l. The first is *confession of sin;* the second is *forgiveness of sin.* In the New Testament, we have the same two-step process described in **1 John 1:9.** Write it out here.

One thing is clear: Nothing got past God.

Liz Curtis Higgs in *Really Bad Girls of the Bible*, page 149

7a. David's story of rebellion, repentance, and restoration is so inspiring for all of us who have fallen short of God's glory (which *is* all of us). But as with all love triangles, this one had two other points to consider: Uriah and Bathsheba. Uriah seems like a Good Guy. Is that how you see him? Why or why not?

b. Perhaps Uriah's only weakness was gullibility. Does it appear that he had a clue what was going on?

c. Read **2 Samuel 12:14.** How was Uriah's death—a direct consequence of David's sin—atoned for?

d. Read **1 John 2:1-2.** What innocent son died so that our own sins would be atoned for?

e. As to Bathsheba—the third point of our marriage triangle—she not only married David and was counted among his wives, but she appears again in Scripture at the close of David's life (**1 Kings 1:28-31**). Read **2 Samuel 12:24.** What clues are we given in this verse that her relationship with David was a solid one?

f. What indication is there that at some point her relationship with God was restored?

g. The first verse of the New Testament, **Matthew 1:1,** reminds us that Jesus was called "the son of David," and in **Matthew 1:6** we see where David falls in the lineage of Christ. Usually only the men were listed. What woman do we find in this verse?

h. How does this passage from the Gospels assure us not only that Bathsheba was forgiven by God but that we can be forgiven as well?

i. Write your own prayer of thanks to our God who uses less-than-perfect people to accomplish his perfect will.

God uses broken people. Sinful people. Less-than-perfect people.

Liz Curtis Higgs in *Really Bad Girls of the Bible*, page 157

8. What's the most important lesson you learned from the soap-opera story of Bathsheba and her king?

6

Just Desserts

Herodias

H er dancing daughter, Salome, whose name isn't even included in the biblical account, may be more famous than she was. But Herodias was the first one to whisper, "Off with his head!" Come observe her odious actions and discover what really pleases God...and what doesn't.

1a. First, let's meet the real John the Baptist, the wilderness preacher whose head Herodias coveted. Read **Luke 1:13-17.** John's life was extraordinary from conception forward. List all the unusual things you can find about this son of Elizabeth and Zechariah.

b. Above all, John's ministry would be one of preparation. Read **Matthew 3:1-6.** What was his message?

c. As a result of John's ministry and message, what two things were people convicted to do?

d. Read **Mark 6:17-20.** Who gave orders to have John the Baptist arrested?

e. According to John the Baptist, what violation had Herod committed?

f. List several things we learn about Herod's wife in **Mark 6:19.**

g. How might these verses from Proverbs suit Herodias?

Proverbs 12:4

Proverbs 27:15-16

h. And what do we learn about Herod in **Mark 6:20?**

i. In a few words, how would you describe the marriage relationship of Herod and Herodias?

j. Reread page 172 of *Really Bad Girls of the Bible*. From your viewpoint, what makes a family dysfunctional?

k. Where do you find manipulation and control at work in **Mark 6:17-20**?

l. Do you ever stumble over control issues in your own relationships? Think of an example and briefly describe it.

m. The following verses urge us to "stand firm" when we meet opposition, which could certainly include a manipulative family member asking us to do something we don't want to do. Make a note or two that sums up what each verse means to you personally.

2 Corinthians 1:21-22

Galatians 5:1

Nefarious women have little use for righteous prophets.

Liz Curtis Higgs in *Really Bad Girls of the Bible*, page 175

2a. Considering her motive for marriage—wealth and prestige—one wonders if Herodias even loved her second husband, Herod Antipas. Read **Mark 6:17** again, and **Mark 6:26.** What seems to be the driving force behind his decisions?

b. From your own observations, what happens when a strong woman marries a strong man?

c. And what happens when a strong woman marries a weak man?

d. Whatever the balance of power in your marriage, what direction do you find in the following verses for facing your particular challenges?

Proverbs 31:10-12

Jeremiah 9:23-24

Romans 15:1

She *nursed* her anger, feeding and tending that volatile emotion to keep it alive.   Liz Curtis Higgs in *Really Bad Girls of the Bible*, page 175

3a. Unlike David with his Plan A, B, and C, Herodias had only one plan. Read **Mark 6:21-24.** Why do you think Herodias used Salome to convey her request instead of simply demanding John's head herself?

b. To one degree or another, Herodias failed in every area of her life. How would you complete the following statements?

Herodias was a failure as a **wife** because...

Herodias was a failure as a **mother** because...

Herodias was a failure as a **queen** because...

Herodias was a failure as a **woman made in the image of God** because...

c. Now to her daughter's character. Read **Proverbs 20:11-12** first. How do those verses suggest a child's character can be measured?

d. In **Mark 6:25** we learn several things about Salome by her actions and by her words. What can you deduce about her simply by reading this verse?

e. It seems she didn't hesitate to deliver her mother's message. What might that tell us about their relationship?

f. Why do you suppose Salome states this as her own request rather than her mother's?

g. Do you think Salome followed in her mother's evil footsteps? Why or why not?

h. For those of us who had poor parental role models, we need to turn elsewhere for wisdom and godly examples. What do the following verses encourage us to do?

Proverbs 22:17-19

3 John 11

Salome's need for adult guidance is our surest sign she was too young to tango.   Liz Curtis Higgs in *Really Bad Girls of the Bible,* page 183

4a. On pages 180-181 of *Really Bad Girls of the Bible,* you'll find a discussion of Salome's infamous dance routine. How do *you* picture her fancy footwork?

b. Be honest: Were *you* surprised—even a little disappointed—that the seven veils turned out to be dramatic license rather than biblical fact? Why or why not?

c. There are two dozen or so references to dancing throughout the Bible. What do the following verses tell you about God's notion of dancing?

Psalm 30:11

Psalm 149:3

Jeremiah 31:4,13

d. Why do you think artists and playwrights—and Christian commentators—put so much emphasis on Salome's supposedly lewd and enticing dance?

e. Are there other activities where we see evil where none is intended?

f. What does that tell us about human nature…that is to say, our own nature?

Revenge beat a deadly rhythm in her dark heart.

Liz Curtis Higgs in *Really Bad Girls of the Bible*, page 177

5a. Read **Luke 3:18-20.** Which activity got John the Baptist locked up in prison—preaching *good* news to the people or delivering *bad* news to Herod?

b. Which message was ultimately more "dangerous" for Herod? Why?

c. Has a brother or sister in Christ ever confronted you about sin in your life? If so, what was your response?

d. Herod's daughter—and his own sin—forced his hand. Read **Mark 6:26-28.** How does the gospel writer describe Herod's reaction to Salome's request?

e. Why couldn't Herod simply refuse his daughter?

f. Not many among us have demanded "Off with his head!" like Herodias did. But that doesn't mean we haven't done some serious damage. Have you ever wounded an enemy's reputation or cut down someone's confidence or undermined a person's convictions or shot down someone's enthusiasm out of spite or a desire for revenge? Describe a specific example.

g. How or why did you convince yourself "she or he deserves this"?

h. How did you feel after you cut that person down to size?

i. Given a second chance, how would you handle it differently? Here are some verses to encourage you the next time you're tempted to take revenge on an "enemy." Jot down a word or two to remind you what each verse has taught you.

Matthew 5:43-45

Romans 12:19-21

Even those cell walls couldn't protect John from his female nemesis. Liz Curtis Higgs in *Really Bad Girls of the Bible,* page 176

6a. What a sad day for the followers of John the Baptist! Read **Matthew 14:12-13a.** How did Jesus respond when he heard about John's execution?

b. What if Jesus had met Herodias? What might he have said to convince her to repent? Perhaps the following verses might sum up his message. Rewrite each verse as a one-sentence statement made directly to her.

Matthew 4:17: "Herodias...

Luke 15:7: "Herodias...

Luke 5:32: "Herodias...

Acts 3:19: "Herodias...

c. Considering her multitude of sins, was it too late for Herodias to repent? for Salome? for Herod? Why or why not?

d. Jesus might respond to Herodias with the very words of **Luke 13:5.** He offers a clear choice: Either one must _____ or one will _____. **Acts 3:19** outlines the benefits of choosing wisely, which are _____ and

_____.

e. Imagine it: The Lord stands ready to forgive even those who murder his servants! He stands ready to hear our repentant cries as well. Take a moment and write a note of thanks to the Lord for his utterly amazing gift of grace.

Sometimes it pays to leave the banquet before the entertainment starts.   Liz Curtis Higgs in *Really Bad Girls of the Bible,* page 184

7a. We have no record of Herodias ever repenting of her sins. Yet surely she wasn't the only citizen of Galilee who despised the righteous John the Baptist. Since her name means "heroic," do you think there were some who saw her as a brave and courageous heroine because she opposed John's teaching? If not, why not?

  b. If so, what might they have admired about her?

  c. If a personality like hers—strong, bold, authoritative, persuasive, single-minded—were submitted to Christ, how might the Lord use such traits for his kingdom?

  d. Unfortunately, that's not how this story ends. **Jude 18-19** might best describe a woman like Herodias. What qualities are listed in those verses that suit her?

e. Are you disappointed that this story doesn't conclude with Herodias coming to a grisly end like Jezebel did? Why do you think Herodias was spared such a death?

f. **Hebrews 4:13** assures us that, despite appearances, nobody gets away with murder. God misses nothing. How does that truth help you release the need to point out the sins of others and focus instead on your own need for repentance?

[Herodias] didn't merely want John executed; she wanted him disgraced and humbled.

Liz Curtis Higgs in *Really Bad Girls of the Bible*, page 183

8. What's the most important lesson you learned from the revenge-driven story of Herodias and her much-manipulated daughter?

7

Veiled Threat

Tamar the Widow

Tamar was one tough bagel. Two dastardly dead husbands didn't stop her, nor did a disgraceful shunning by her in-laws. Yet, when her story was said and done, she had what she wanted, what Judah wanted, *and* what God wanted: a son whose name would be counted among those in the lineage of Christ. Good or bad…what a woman!

1a. Marriage in the days of the patriarchs had much more to do with land and loot than it did with love. But Judah's marriage to the daughter of Shua—Bethshua—wasn't typical. Read **Genesis 28:1.** According to Judah's grandfather, Isaac, what kind of woman did *not* make a good bride?

b. Now read **Genesis 38:2.** *Uh-oh.* What kind of woman did Judah choose?

c. Judah—son of Jacob, grandson of Isaac, great-grandson of Abraham —*knew* better than to marry someone of a different faith. Why do you think he did so?

d. What command does the Lord give his people concerning marriage in **2 Corinthians 6:14**?

e. Read **Genesis 38:6.** Who did the matchmaking here?

f. It seems the marriage didn't last very long. Read **Genesis 38:7.** What was the result of his despicable conduct?

g. In **Genesis 38:8,** a second marriage takes place. Who was Tamar paired with next, and for what purpose?

h. Read page 207 in *Really Bad Girls of the Bible* for a description of levirate marriage. How did this law benefit a childless widow like Tamar?

i. What do the following verses tell us about God and his laws?

Leviticus 18:4-5

Deuteronomy 10:12-13

j. Judah, son of Jacob, knew God's laws—read **Psalm 147:19-20** for proof—yet Judah and his sons demonstrate what happens when God's laws are ignored. Why do we chafe against God's laws, when we know they are for our own good?

That's the key with this story: understanding what kind of rules and regs the woman was up against.

Liz Curtis Higgs in *Really Bad Girls of the Bible,* page 204

2a. Tamar's first husband, the evil Er, was dead, and in accordance with the law she married Onan. Our story continues in **Genesis 38:9-10.** The NIV translation calls Onan "wicked," just like his older brother. What other words might you use to describe him, based on both his *motives* and his *actions* here?

b. In both **Genesis 38:7** and **Genesis 38:10** it is clear that God deemed Judah's sons worthy of death for their wickedness. Write out the psalmist's request of God in **Psalm 119:126.**

c. How do you reconcile a God of judgment with a God of grace? Read **Psalm 111:7-8,** then answer from your heart.

d. It's clear that God saw Tamar's misery. How might the following verses fit the widow Tamar in her bereft situation?

Job 36:6

Psalm 68:5

Onan...was many things. "Considerate" was not one of them.

Liz Curtis Higgs in *Really Bad Girls of the Bible*, page 207

3a. Two sons dead and still no grandsons. Judah was *not* happy. Read **Genesis 38:11.** What motivated Judah's decision to send Tamar home?

b. Turn to page 209 of *Really Bad Girls of the Bible.* What were the "three strikes" against Tamar?

(1)

(2)

(3)

c. According to God's law in **Deuteronomy 25:5,** was Judah justified in keeping his third son, Shelah, away from Tamar?

d. How do you view Judah's "protection" of Shelah—was it a sin or parental love in action?

e. Too bad we never hear from his wife Bethshua in these scenes! If you are a mother, can you describe a time when you behaved irrationally to protect your child?

f. Judah brought Tamar into his household, accepted responsibility for her—then sent her packing. What does **1 Timothy 5:8** tell us about taking care of family members?

g. If providing for your relatives is an issue for you right now—grown children returning home (or constantly begging for money!), aging parents or grandparents needing care—what is the most difficult aspect of that situation for you?

h. Despite the challenges, how can you avoid following in Judah's footsteps?

[Tamar] wasn't homeless, but she *was* rootless, with no provision made for her future.

Liz Curtis Higgs in *Really Bad Girls of the Bible*, page 209

4a. We learned in **Genesis 38:1-2** that Judah's friend Hirah introduced him to Bethshua, Judah's Canaanite bride. Well, Hirah's back again in **Genesis 38:12.** Hirah was the kind of friend Paul wrote about in the New Testament. Write out **1 Corinthians 15:33.**

b. How might that verse describe the friendship of Judah and Hirah?

c. Because of her in-limbo status, Tamar may not have had many friends, but *somebody* kept her informed. Read **Genesis 38:13-14.** What did she wear…and why?

d. Where did she sit…and why?

e. Read **Genesis 38:15.** How can it be that Judah didn't recognize his own daughter-in-law? Come up with as many possible reasons as you can.

f. **Genesis 38:16-18** makes short work of their exchange of goods for services rendered. Why do you think Judah was willing to pay such an outrageous price?

g. Note in verse 18 we are told about the pregnancy right away, even though it would be some time before Tamar would know. What purpose might there be for including it here?

h. What's the significance of **Genesis 38:19?**

i. Reread the fictional account of Tammy in Vegas on page 200 of *Really Bad Girls of the Bible.* Who committed the greater sin— Tammy/Tamar the tempting prostitute or Judd/Judah the eager paying customer?

j. Can sins be "graded" as such? Does God view sin in categories—bad, terrible, worse? Why or why not?

k. How might **James 2:10** help you answer that question?

> Judah went off to shear his sheep, but he was the one about to get fleeced!
>
> Liz Curtis Higgs in Really Bad Girls of the Bible, page 210

5a. Some see Tamar as a harlot, others a heroine. Is there anything about Tamar you appreciate? Her creativity, perhaps, or her shrewdness? What positive words come to mind?

b. How might she have justified her deliberate, deceptive actions?

c. Based on the scriptural account, Tamar was innocent of any intentional wrongdoing *except* for her sexual encounter by the side of the road with Judah, her one unrighteous act. So…do you see her as a true "Bad Girl"? Why or why not?

d. After studying all these women, this might be a good time to ask: What *is* your definition of a "Bad Girl"?

e. How might **Ephesians 5:1-3** help you identify behaviors that are out of bounds for a Good Girl?

f. The NIV translation cautions against "even a hint" of immorality or impurity. Examine your life closely for such "hints." If there are things that need to be eliminated, dear sister, what is the first step you need to take, practically speaking?

Tamar felt she had no choice but this one because of the poor choice Judah had made.

Liz Curtis Higgs in *Really Bad Girls of the Bible*, page 211

6a. After Tamar's "Bad Girl" moment, things started heating up three months later. Read **Genesis 38:24.** Why do you think she is charged with *prostitution* and not, say, adultery or fornication?

b. What justification do you suppose Judah offered for the harsh sentence of death by burning rather than stoning? In the middle of page 218 of *Really Bad Girls of the Bible*, I suggest four reasons why Judah demanded she be burned. Write down the one that seems most likely and explain why.

c. Have you ever, even for an angry moment, wished someone were out of your life for good? If so, did you say it—or only think it?

d. What does **James 1:19-20** teach us about anger?

e. Anytime we are tempted to justify our sinful actions, **1 Corinthians 4:4** is a good reminder. Write out the verse here.

She kept a cool head and focused her eyes on the prize: children in her womb.

Liz Curtis Higgs in *Really Bad Girls of the Bible*, page 214

7a. Read **Genesis 38:25-26.** What advantage might there have been for Tamar to wait until the last minute to address Judah?

b. Look at her two statements in verse 25. The first is straightforward, with no name implied. What's different about her second statement?

c. What do you think Tamar was trying to accomplish by handling things the way she did?

d. Notice what Judah does *not* say. He does not speak his guilt aloud. What confession *does* Judah make?

e. Why was it important that Judah not sleep with Tamar again?

f. Judah said Tamar was "more righteous" than he was, to which I wrote on page 220, "'more' right isn't the same as 'all' right." What do you think an *all*-righteous Tamar might have done differently?

g. According to **Genesis 38:27-30,** she gave birth to two sons. Those twin boys were not an accident of nature. What do you think they signified?

h. What purpose do you believe God had for including Tamar the Canaanite and Judah the Israelite in the lineage of Christ?

i. What hope might you offer a woman with a checkered story like Tamar's?

j. Do you, like me, struggle when stories in the Bible don't seem logical, or we really *can't* see God's hand in the situation, even though we know it's there? Read the following passages and jot down how each one encourages you to believe that, unfathomable as his ways may be, God is in charge.

Romans 8:28

Colossians 2:2-3

Hebrews 6:13-18

No matter what the circumstances of our conception–God is sovereign.   Liz Curtis Higgs in *Really Bad Girls of the Bible*, page 215

8. What's the most important lesson you learned from the uneasy, yet ultimately redemptive story of Tamar the widow?

Tears of a Clown

The Bleeding Woman

More than once I've been asked why I chose this title for our afflicted woman's story. Not because her illness was laughable, I can promise you that! I was thinking of the old hit song *Tears of a Clown,* recorded by Smokey Robinson and (drumroll, please) *the Miracles.* As a woman who has laughed on the outside while crying on the inside, I understand something about masking pain beneath a painted smile. I hoped that memorable song title would suit our story of Vera the Clown—and Veronica the woman—very well.

1a. The chapter opens with a quote from Marcel Proust that captures the paradoxical truth of suffering. Copy that quote here as you let the weight of his words sink in.

b. Do you agree with Proust? Why or why not?

c. In what circumstances have you personally experienced suffering "to the full"?

d. Was there a "healing" of sorts that took place for you? If so, how... and when?

e. What do these verses tell us about the (often unexpected) benefits of suffering?

Romans 5:3-4

1 Peter 2:19

f. When he walked this earth, Jesus was unquestionably a healer. Read **Matthew 4:24.** What are some of the human conditions Jesus healed?

    (1)   (4)

    (2)   (5)

    (3)

g. **Matthew 15:30-31** adds to that list...

    (6)   (8)

    (7)   (9)

h. Note the *result* of those healings, stated in the last phrase of verse 31.

i. Jesus had no qualms about touching those who were "unclean"— whether from leprosy, skin lesions, or "female problems," as this woman had. How do you handle yourself around people who have life-threatening illnesses such as cancer or AIDS or physical challenges such as blindness or missing limbs? Being totally honest with yourself, underline any of the following possibilities that accurately describe your reactions, internal and external. If none of these quite fit, describe your reaction in the space provided.

    • I feel a tiny bit of inner revulsion.
    • I overcompensate with outward enthusiasm.
    • I try to ignore their situation.
    • I address their situation head-on and ask questions.
    • I try to find practical ways to be helpful.
    • Or I...

j. Mentally sift through your past experiences, good and bad, then read
    the following verses and jot down the advice you find there concern-
    ing how we should treat others.

John 13:15

Acts 10:28

Galatians 6:2

k. Jesus surely must have been more repulsed by what was in men's
    hearts than what was wrong with their bodies, yet he cared enough to
    reach out to them, even as he reaches out to us. Practically speaking,
    how might you follow Jesus' example and make everyone you meet,
    regardless of his or her physical or spiritual challenges, feel loved and
    accepted?

We are, every one of us, sick.
Liz Curtis Higgs in *Really Bad Girls of the Bible*, page 236

2a. Read **Mark 5:25-26.** We don't know this woman's name, but we do know some critical details about her life. How long had she suffered…and what was the result?

b. One of this woman's admirable qualities was her long-term willingness to keep asking for help. What do the following verses teach us about waiting and persevering?

Psalm 27:14

Ecclesiastes 7:8

Hebrews 10:36

c. What if instead of healing her, Jesus had given her sufficient strength to bear the pain another dozen years? Would that also have been a form of grace? Why or why not?

d. Have you observed or experienced a situation when God answered a prayer for healing in that way—with courage to go on instead of a cure? Describe what you saw or felt, and what you learned.

e. The apostle Paul struggled with an unnamed "thorn in his flesh"— probably physical in nature, though we are not told. Read **2 Corinthians 12:7-10.** After Paul pleaded three times for the Lord to take it away, how did God respond?

f. And what was Paul's victorious conclusion?

g. Think of some area of your life where you've faced disappointment or perhaps have sensed a "no" from God. Now rewrite Paul's response from verses 9 and 10 in your own words, personalizing it to fit your own challenge, beginning with this statement: "Therefore I will..."

Jesus didn't take money for his miracles.

Liz Curtis Higgs in *Really Bad Girls of the Bible*, page 236

3a. Reread the fictional story of Veronica on page 232 of *Really Bad Girls of the Bible*. What compelled this young woman forward toward the hem of his garment?

b. Now read the biblical version in **Mark 5:27-28.** Spiritually speaking, wrap yourself in this woman's tunic. Page 242 in *Really Bad Girls of the Bible* may help to set the scene firmly in your imagination. On that long journey to Capernaum, what do you suppose she told herself?

c. Where did she get the emotional fortitude to keep putting one foot in front of the other? Read **1 Peter 1:8-9** for one possibility. Might there be others?

d. Is the fact that she'd even *survived* twelve years of nonstop bleeding a
miracle to you? Why or why not?

e. **Galatians 3:4-5** asks two questions. How might this woman have
answered them…and how would you answer them based on your
own life?

Her Possible Answers	**Your Answers**
(1)	(1)
(2)	(2)

A dozen years of never being touched by anyone. Ever.
Liz Curtis Higgs in *Really Bad Girls of the Bible*, page 239

4a. Read **Mark 5:28** again. Touching someone, however lightly or inno-
cently, is a powerful means of communication. Why do you suppose
she thought merely touching him would be sufficient for her healing?

b. And why do you suppose she touched his *garment* rather than, say, his hand?

c. Why did she approach him from the back rather than walk up to him as others did?

d. How did Jesus heal people in the following verses?

	Illness	Method of Healing
Mark 7:32-35		
Luke 5:12-13		
John 9:1-3,6-7		

e. Was there a particular *significance* in the ways that Jesus healed—with his hands, his words, water, mud, etc.—or just variety?

f. How can we "touch the hem of his garment" today? What might **Philippians 2:1-4** offer as a possible answer?

g. Now let's see what happened when she touched his garment. Read **Mark 5:29,** then write down all the words that point to a dramatic change taking place.

h. Do those words suggest to you coincidence or miracle? What makes you say that?

To their first-century way of thinking, sin and disease walked hand in hand.   Liz Curtis Higgs in *Really Bad Girls of the Bible*, page 240

5a. The woman was *not* the only one who knew something had happened, though. Read **Mark 5:30.** Who else knew, and how soon did he realize it?

b. What question did he ask?

c. If he, being the Son of God, already knew the answer, why do you think he asked the question?

d. Read **Mark 5:33.** What might have prompted her to come forward? Fear? Gratitude? What?

e. And what does the Scripture say she told Jesus?

f. It's clear that Jesus wanted everyone to hear the woman's testimony. Can you think of some reasons why he might have done that? What were the possible benefits...

for the woman?

for Jesus?

for the community?

for the disciples?

g. **Romans 1:16** explains *why* we tell people "the whole truth," and **1 John 5:11-12** explains *what* we tell people. If you have heard someone share a testimony of his or her faith experience, what effect did it have on your own spiritual life?

h. No matter how dramatic or commonplace you think your personal testimony is, write a three-sentence story of how you came to know Christ—or had a life-changing experience at some point in your Christian walk.

i. Writing it is one thing. Sharing it aloud is another. If the idea of verbally sharing your testimony makes you "tremble with fear" like our woman in Mark 5, you're not alone. Paul confessed to his audience in Corinth that he was nervous about speaking to them. Read **1 Corinthians 2:1-5.** How did Paul describe his emotional state?

j. What did Paul limit himself to telling them?

k. What did his weakness demonstrate?

1. Encouraged by Paul's example, think of someone you need to share your story with this week, someone who might be as surprised as these onlookers were that day long ago in Capernaum. That person's name is: _____. What steps will you need to take to make sure you connect with them this week?

Bad or good, she'd come all that way in search of a miracle.

Liz Curtis Higgs in *Really Bad Girls of the Bible*, page 242

6a. This woman's story is one of many in the Gospels that describe the miracles Christ performed during his short earthly ministry. But God has always been in the miracle business. Read **Psalm 77:11-14.** What attributes of God did the psalmist describe?

b. How would *you* define a miracle?

c. Do you see miracles, or evidence of God's power, happening around you today? If so, describe one. If not, are we past the time of miracles?

d. Have you seen miracles become a divisive issue in the church today? Why might that be the case?

e. Read **Mark 11:22-24.** How do you reconcile these words of Jesus— and miraculous stories like the bleeding woman's healing—with your own day-to-day experience of people praying for healing who are not healed?

f. Does this challenge your faith? If doubts have surfaced, how has God answered them and assured you of his love in any circumstance?

g. How might **Hebrews 13:8** encourage you?

h. **Mark 5:34** records Jesus' final words to this woman once her healing was complete and her testimony spoken. What endearing term did he call her?

i. Imagine how this sounded to her after years in exile! Is there a pet name or endearment you would take comfort in hearing the Lord speak to you?

j. What did Jesus credit for her healing?

k. Why do you think he said that, instead of "God has healed you"?

l. He sent her off with a two-part benediction:

    (1)

    (2)

m. Now she knew that not only had the bleeding—the symptom of her disease—stopped, but that she also was healed and the disease itself was gone forever. Why was that a critical distinction?

When you are ready for God, *God is more than ready for you.*
Liz Curtis Higgs in *Really Bad Girls of the Bible*, page 243

7a. The bleeding woman's story falls right in the middle of another desperate situation introduced in **Mark 5:21-24** and concluded in **Mark 5:35-43.** Do you suppose Jairus hopped from one foot to the other, waiting for Jesus to finish with the bleeding woman so his daughter's needs could be met? After all, wasn't he there first? Why do you think Jesus made this father wait?

b. And what of our bleeding sister, waiting twelve years to be healed?
   Do you imagine she ever ran out of patience with God? What would
   you have been saying to God if you were in her place?

c. What does **Jude 21** encourage us to do?

d. But waiting is hard! Read **Romans 8:25.** If you've ever waited for
   God to pay attention to your requests, what did you learn during the
   waiting process?

e. How did others console you?

f. And how would you *like* to have been consoled and encouraged?

g. **Colossians 1:10-12** reminds us of what the Christian life is really all about—not perfect health and endless wealth as the world defines them but our heavenly inheritance. Note the "to-do" activities suggested in each verse.

Verse 10

Verse 11

Verse 12

h. On page 252 of *Really Bad Girls of the Bible,* our concluding lesson is "Faith is a gift." In the book I list a progression of gifts from God, to which we then respond. Write those gifts in the space provided as they appear in the book, then look up the corresponding verse that demonstrates that truth and summarize it below in your own words.

He gives us...
John 6:44

He gives us...
Ephesians 2:8

He gives us...
1 Corinthians 12:3

He gives us...
Ephesians 1:5-7

He gives us...
John 17:2-3

Thank you, Lord for the indescribable, irrevocable gift of *you!*

Not only was the blood gone, her *shame* was gone as well.
Liz Curtis Higgs in *Really Bad Girls of the Bible,* page 247

8. What's the most important lesson you learned from the miraculous story of the Bleeding Woman?

A Last Word from Liz

What a bevy of Bad Girls you've studied! Bless you for taking the time, sis.

If this workbook expanded your understanding of the Bible and your appreciation for the timeless truth of God's Word, my prayers have been answered. I hope you learned a bit about yourself as well. When the truth gets inside you, it seldom sits still! "For the word of God is living and active. Sharper than any double-edged sword, it penetrates even to dividing soul and spirit, joints and marrow; it judges the thoughts and attitudes of the heart" (Hebrews 4:12).

May your heart not only be gently cut open, dear one, but also washed clean.

Such wonderful encouragers I had while writing this workbook. Glenna Salsbury, a dear sister in Christ and even dearer friend, contributed several insightful questions. Lynn Reece, another Bible study veteran, provided helpful feedback. Once again, Rebecca Price, Laura Barker, Carol Bartley, and Stephanie Terry read the finished product and offered excellent direction. And I can never praise enough my dear hubby, Bill, who brought his seminary-trained skills to my meager manuscript and made sure it was as accurate as humanly possible.

If you haven't already studied *Bad Girls of the Bible,* you'll find the best-selling book, workbook, and video waiting at a bookstore near you, as well as my third book in the Bad Girls collection, *Unveiling Mary Magdalene.* I'd love to have another opportunity to study God's Word with you!

Although I've tallied more than fifteen hundred speaking engagements and twenty-six published books to date, the Lord still has *much* to teach me. Stubborn as I am, this could take awhile. Kind sisters in Christ (like you!) are a key element of that learning process, and I'm truly blessed when readers find a moment to write me at:

Liz Curtis Higgs
P.O. Box 43577
Louisville, KY 40253-0577

Or visit my Web site:
www.LizCurtisHiggs.com

Until we meet again—across the page, online, or in person—grow in grace, girlfriend!